I0012263

SQL Beginners Guide

The Beginner's Path to SQL, with Unveiling the Secrets of SQL for beginners,

By Frank T Gibbs

All rights reserved. No part of this publication may be reproduced, distributed, or transmitted in any form or by any means, including photocopying, recording, or other electronic or mechanical methods, without the prior written permission of the publisher, except in the case of brief quotations embodied in critical reviews and certain other noncommercial uses permitted by copyright law.

Copyright © Frank T. Gibbs, 2023.

Chapter 1:

Introduction to SQL and Relational Databases

1. The Importance of Managing Data

In the modern digital era, data has become an invaluable asset for organizations across various industries. Effective management and organization of data are critical for businesses to make informed decisions, gain valuable insights, and maintain a competitive advantage. This is where databases play a vital role. Databases offer a structured and efficient way to store, retrieve, and manage large volumes of data. Among the different types of databases, relational databases have emerged as the most popular and widely used solution.

2. Understanding Databases and their Structure

A database is a collection of related data that is organized and structured to facilitate efficient storage, retrieval, and manipulation. It serves as a central repository for storing various types of information, such as customer details, product inventory, financial records, and more. Databases consist of tables, which are structured into rows and columns. Each row represents a record or an instance of data, while each column represents a specific attribute or field.

3. Exploring the Components of a Relational Database

Relational databases are based on the relational model, which was proposed by Edgar F. Codd in the 1970s. This model organizes data into tables that are related to each other through common attributes. Let's dive deeper into the key components of a relational database:

Key components of relational database

a. Tables:
Tables are the fundamental building blocks of a relational database. They consist of rows and columns,

representing entities and attributes, respectively. Each table has a unique name and a predefined structure.

b. Primary Key:
A primary key is a unique identifier for each record in a table. It ensures the uniqueness and integrity of the data. Typically, a primary key is a column or a combination of columns that uniquely identify a record.

c. Foreign Key:
A foreign key is a column in one table that refers to the primary key of another table. It establishes relationships between tables and enables data integrity and consistency.

d. Relationships:
Relationships define how tables are connected to each other. The most common types of relationships are one-to-one, one-to-many, and many-to-many. These relationships help in retrieving and manipulating data across multiple tables.

4. Introducing SQL and Its Purpose

Structured Query Language (SQL) is a programming language specifically designed for managing and manipulating relational databases. SQL provides a standardized way to interact with databases, allowing users to define, manipulate, and query data. It offers a wide range of capabilities, including creating and modifying database structures, inserting and updating data, and retrieving data based on specific criteria.

5. Differentiating SQL from Other Query Languages

While SQL is the most popular query language for relational databases, it's essential to understand its differences from other query languages.

Here are some key distinctions:

a. Procedural vs. Declarative:
SQL is a declarative language, meaning you specify what you want, and the database management system (DBMS) determines how to retrieve the data. In

contrast, procedural languages, such as Java or Python, require you to define the steps and logic for data retrieval.

b. Set-based Operations:
SQL operates on sets of data, allowing you to perform operations on multiple records at once. This makes SQL highly efficient for handling large volumes of data. In contrast, other languages often operate on individual records, leading to less efficient processing.

c. Data Manipulation Focus:
SQL is primarily focused on manipulating and retrieving data from databases. It provides powerful querying capabilities, data filtering, sorting, aggregation, and more. Other languages may have broader applications beyond database operations.

6 Setting Up an Environment for SQL Practice

To practice SQL, you need an environment that includes a relational database management system (RDBMS) and a tool to interact with the database.

Let's explore the common steps to set up an SQL environment:

a. Choose an RDBMS:
Select a relational database management system that suits your needs. Popular options include MySQL, PostgreSQL, Oracle Database, and Microsoft SQL Server.

b. Install the RDBMS:
Download and install the chosen RDBMS on your computer or use a cloud-based solution.

c. Choose a SQL Client:
Select a tool or client application to interact with the database. Examples include MySQL Workbench, pgAdmin, SQL Developer, and SQL Server Management Studio.

d. Connect to the Database:
Configure the SQL client to connect to the database by providing the necessary connection details, such as server address, port, username, and password.

e. Create a Sample Database:
Once connected, you can create a sample database to practice SQL queries. You can find tutorials or use sample databases provided by the RDBMS vendors.

f. Practice SQL Queries:
Start practicing SQL by writing and executing queries in the SQL client. Familiarize yourself with basic query syntax, data manipulation statements (e.g., SELECT, INSERT, UPDATE, DELETE), and data definition statements (e.g., CREATE TABLE, ALTER TABLE).

g. Explore Advanced Concepts: As you gain proficiency in SQL, you can explore advanced concepts such as joins, subqueries, indexes, views, and stored procedures. These concepts will enhance your ability to work with complex databases and optimize performance.

To cut it short. In this introductory chapter, we have explored the fundamental concepts of SQL and relational databases. We have highlighted the importance of managing data effectively and how databases provide a structured approach to store and retrieve information. The key components of a relational database, including tables, primary keys, foreign keys, and relationships, have been discussed.

SQL has been introduced as the standard query language for managing relational databases, emphasizing its purpose and distinguishing it from other languages. Lastly, we have outlined the steps to set up an SQL environment for practice. In the following chapters, we will delve deeper into SQL syntax, querying techniques, and advanced database management concepts to enhance your understanding and proficiency in SQL.

Chapter 2:

Getting Started with SQL Queries

Welcome to the world of SQL! Structured Query Language (SQL) is a powerful tool for managing and manipulating data in relational databases. Whether you are a beginner or an experienced developer, understanding how to write SQL queries is an essential skill for working with databases. In this chapter, we will delve into the basics of writing SQL queries and explore strategies for formulating simple SELECT statements to retrieve data from a database.

1: Constructing a Basic SELECT Statement

To get started with SQL queries, let's first understand the anatomy of a basic SELECT statement. The SELECT statement is the core of querying in SQL and is used to retrieve data from one or more tables in a database. Here's a general structure of a SELECT statement:

```sql
SELECT column1, column2, ...
FROM table_name;
```

In this structure, `SELECT` is a keyword that indicates that we want to retrieve data, followed by a comma-separated list of columns we want to retrieve data from. The `FROM` keyword specifies the table or tables from which we want to retrieve the data.

For example, let's say we have a table called `employees` with columns `id`, `name`, `age`, and `salary`. To retrieve all the data from this table, we can write the following SELECT statement:

```sql
SELECT * FROM employees;
```

The asterisk (*) is a wildcard character that represents all columns in the table. This statement will retrieve all the columns and all the rows from the `employees` table.

2: Retrieving Data from a Single Table

Now that we understand the basic structure of a SELECT statement, let's dive deeper into retrieving data from a single table. SQL provides various clauses and operators that allow us to filter, sort, and manipulate data.

a) Filtering Data using WHERE Clause

The WHERE clause allows us to filter data based on specific conditions. It enables us to retrieve only the rows that meet the specified criteria. Here's an example:

```sql
SELECT *
FROM employees
WHERE age > 30;
```

In this example, we are retrieving all the columns and rows from the `employees` table where the age is greater than 30. The WHERE clause specifies the condition, and only the rows that satisfy the condition will be returned.

b) Sorting Data with ORDER BY

The ORDER BY clause is used to sort the retrieved data in ascending or descending order based on one or more columns. Here's an example:

```sql
SELECT *
FROM employees
ORDER BY salary DESC;
```

In this example, we are retrieving all the columns and rows from the `employees` table and sorting them in descending order based on the `salary` column. The `DESC` keyword specifies the descending order.

3: Limiting and Offsetting Results

Sometimes, we may only want to retrieve a subset of rows or skip a certain number of rows from the beginning of the result set. SQL provides two useful clauses for accomplishing this: LIMIT and OFFSET.

a) LIMITing Results

The LIMIT clause allows us to limit the number of rows returned in the result set. Here's an example:

```sql
SELECT *
FROM employees
LIMIT 10;
```

In this example, we are retrieving the first 10 rows from the `employees` table. The result set will contain only 10 rows, regardless of how many rows exist in the table.

b) OFFSETting Results

The OFFSET clause is used in conjunction with the LIMIT clause to skip a specified number of rows before starting to retrieve the result set. Here's an example:

```sql
SELECT *
FROM employees
LIMIT 10 OFFSET 20;
```

In this example, we are retrieving 10 rows from the `employees` table starting from the 21st row. The result set will skip the first 20 rows and retrieve the subsequent 10 rows.

4: Using Wildcard Characters and Logical Operators

a) Wildcard Characters

Wildcard characters are used in conjunction with the LIKE operator to perform pattern matching in SQL queries. The two commonly used wildcard characters are the percent sign (%) and underscore (_).

- The percent sign (%) represents zero, one, or multiple characters.
- The underscore (_) represents a single character.

For example, let's say we want to retrieve all the employees whose names start with "J". We can use the following query:

```sql
SELECT *
FROM employees
WHERE name LIKE 'J%';
```

In this example, the '%' wildcard matches any number of characters after the letter 'J', effectively retrieving all the employees whose names start with 'J'.

b) Logical Operators

Logical operators such as AND, OR, and NOT can be used to combine multiple conditions in a WHERE clause. Here's an example:

```sql
SELECT *
FROM employees
WHERE age > 30 AND salary > 50000;
```

In this example, we are retrieving all the employees from the `employees` table whose age is greater than 30 and salary is greater than 50,000. The AND operator ensures that both conditions must be true for a row to be included in the result set.

In the end I would like to say a big Congratulations to you! You've learned the basics of writing SQL queries to retrieve data from a database. In this chapter, we covered constructing a basic SELECT statement, retrieving data from a single table, filtering data using the WHERE clause, sorting data with ORDER BY, limiting and offsetting results, and using wildcard characters and logical operators. With this knowledge, you are well-equipped to start exploring the vast world of SQL querying and unlock the power to extract meaningful insights from databases.

In the next chapter, we will delve further into advanced SQL querying techniques, including joining multiple tables, aggregating data, and utilizing subqueries. Stay tuned for an exciting journey of mastering SQL!

Chapter 3:

Advanced Querying Techniques

The art of querying databases is akin to unlocking a treasure trove of knowledge. In previous chapters, we explored the fundamentals of SQL and learned how to retrieve data from a single table. Now, it's time to delve into the realm of advanced querying techniques. Brace yourself, for we are about to embark on a journey that will empower you to harness the full potential of SQL.

1. Joining Tables: Uniting Data Dimensions

In the vast landscape of databases, information is often spread across multiple tables. Joining tables allows us to bring together related data, enabling comprehensive analysis and insights. SQL offers different types of joins, each with its own purpose:

a. Inner Join:

This type of join combines records from two tables based on a specified condition, returning only the matching rows. It helps us uncover relationships between entities and paints a clearer picture of the data landscape.

b. Left Join:

By utilizing this join, we retrieve all records from the left table and only the matching records from the right table. This is particularly useful when we want to include all records from one table, regardless of whether there is a match in the other table.

c. Right Join:

The right join is the opposite of the left join. It returns all records from the right table and only the matching records from the left table.

d. Full Outer Join:

This powerful join type retrieves all records from both tables, merging them together and returning NULL values when there are no matches.

Understanding the nuances of joins is paramount to effectively exploring relationships within a database.

2. Subqueries: Unleashing the Power of Complexity

When the questions we pose to a database become more intricate, subqueries come to our rescue. A subquery is a query nested within another query, allowing us to perform complex data retrieval and analysis. This technique provides flexibility and empowers us to tackle even the most intricate data scenarios.

With subqueries, we can construct queries that answer questions like: "Which customers made a purchase greater than the average purchase value?" or "What are the top-selling products among customers who have made more than five purchases?" By breaking down complex problems into manageable parts, subqueries enable us to unravel the secrets hidden within our data.

3. Aggregate Functions: Summarizing the Story

As we traverse the realm of advanced querying, we encounter scenarios where we need to summarize and analyze data. Enter aggregate functions, the tools that enable us to distill vast amounts of information into meaningful insights. Here are some fundamental aggregate functions:

a. SUM: This function allows us to calculate the sum of a numerical column, enabling us to find the total sales, expenses, or any other cumulative value.

b. COUNT: With the count function, we can determine the number of records or non-null values within a column, providing us with vital statistics for our analysis.

c. AVG: The average function calculates the average value of a column, helping us understand the typical or expected value.

d. MIN and MAX: These functions return the minimum and maximum values in a column, respectively. They assist us in identifying outliers and extreme data points.

e. GROUP_CONCAT: This function concatenates values from multiple rows into a single string, facilitating the creation of informative reports.

By employing these aggregate functions, we can unravel the hidden patterns and trends residing within our data.

4. GROUP BY and HAVING: Unraveling Insights

In the realm of data analysis, grouping and filtering data are essential techniques. The GROUP BY clause allows us to group rows based on specific columns, while the HAVING clause filters the grouped data based on conditions. Together, they offer a powerful mechanism for diving deep into the data.

With GROUP BY, we can answer questions such as: "What is the total revenue for each product category?" or "How many customers fall into different age groups?" This allows us to discern patterns, detect anomalies, and draw meaningful conclusions.

The HAVING clause, on the other hand, adds another layer of analysis by enabling us to filter the grouped data based on aggregated values. It allows us to focus on specific subsets of data that meet particular conditions. For instance, we can filter only those product categories with total sales exceeding a certain threshold.

By utilizing GROUP BY and HAVING, we navigate through the labyrinth of data, extracting valuable insights that help drive informed decision-making.

5. The Enigma of NULL Values

In the realm of databases, the concept of NULL values often perplexes even seasoned SQL practitioners. NULL represents the absence of a value or an unknown value. Handling NULL values is crucial to ensuring accurate and reliable results in our queries.

When dealing with NULL values, we encounter challenges such as handling calculations, comparisons, and data integrity. It is important to understand how NULL values propagate through our queries and how they interact with aggregate functions, joins, and filtering conditions.

By mastering the art of handling NULL values, we gain a deeper understanding of our data and eliminate the potential pitfalls that may arise from their presence.

As we conclude this chapter on advanced querying techniques, you now possess a formidable arsenal to tackle the most intricate data scenarios. Joining tables, harnessing the power of subqueries, summarizing data with aggregate functions, grouping and filtering data, and comprehending the enigma of NULL values have unlocked a world of possibilities within your reach.

Remember, querying databases is not merely about extracting information; it is about extracting insights, patterns, and stories that empower informed decision-making. Embrace the complexity, embrace the challenges, and unleash the power of advanced querying techniques to unravel the hidden truths within your data.

In the next chapter, we shall embark on a new quest, exploring the art of database optimization and performance tuning. Prepare yourself for a journey that will unlock the true potential of your databases and elevate your SQL skills to new heights.

Chapter 4:

Manipulating Data with SQL

In the vast realm of databases, the ability to manipulate data is akin to wielding a master craftsman's tools. With SQL, you possess the power to shape, mold, and breathe life into your data. In this chapter, we will embark on a journey through the art of data manipulation, exploring the techniques that allow you to add, update, and delete data within a database. Prepare to uncover the secrets of manipulating data with SQL and unleash the full potential of your databases.

1. Inserting Data: Seeding the Foundation

Every great database begins with data. To populate your tables with meaningful information, you must become adept at inserting data. SQL provides a straightforward and powerful syntax for this task. Let's explore the various ways you can insert data into your tables:

a. Single-Row Insert:
This method allows you to insert a single row of data into a table. You provide the values for each column, carefully aligning them with the table's schema.

b. Multi-Row Insert:
When dealing with larger datasets, you can utilize a multi-row insert statement to efficiently add multiple rows at once. By specifying the values for each row in a concise format, you streamline the insertion process.

c. Inserting Data from Another Table: SQL enables you to insert data into a table directly from another table, leveraging the power of subqueries. This technique allows for dynamic data population and data transformation during the insertion process.

By mastering the art of inserting data, you lay the foundation for the transformative power of data manipulation.

2. Updating Records: Refining the Details

In the ever-evolving landscape of data, updates are inevitable. SQL equips us with the tools to modify existing records, ensuring the accuracy and relevance of our data. Here are the key elements of updating records:

  a. UPDATE Statement:
The UPDATE statement forms the backbone of record updates in SQL. It allows you to specify the table, set the new values for the desired columns, and apply filtering conditions to determine which rows to update.

  b. SET Clause:
Within the UPDATE statement, the SET clause enables you to assign new values to the columns you wish to update. By carefully crafting this clause, you can fine-tune your data to reflect the latest information.

  c. WHERE Clause:
The WHERE clause plays a pivotal role in record updates, allowing you to define the filtering conditions that determine which rows to modify. It empowers you

to selectively update specific subsets of data, ensuring precise control over the changes.

With the power of updates at your disposal, you can seamlessly refine the details of your database, keeping it in sync with the ever-evolving reality it represents.

3. Deleting Data: Taming the Overgrowth

As data accumulates, it becomes necessary to prune the excess and remove obsolete or erroneous information. SQL provides the means to achieve this through the deletion of data. Let's explore the art of deleting data:

a. DELETE Statement:
The DELETE statement is SQL's weapon of choice for removing data from tables. By specifying the table and applying filtering conditions, you can selectively remove rows that meet certain criteria.

b. WHERE Clause:
As with updates, the WHERE clause proves invaluable when deleting data. It enables you to define the

conditions that determine which rows to delete, allowing for precise control over the deletion process.

c. TRUNCATE Statement:

In some cases, you may wish to remove all data from a table quickly. The TRUNCATE statement allows for the removal of all rows within a table, resetting it to an empty state. It offers a faster and more efficient alternative to deleting rows individually.

By mastering the art of deletion, you ensure that your database remains lean, organized, and free from the clutter of outdated or irrelevant information.

4. Combining Data Manipulation Operations: Unleashing the Power

The true power of SQL lies not only in the individual data manipulation operations but also in the ability to combine them. SQL enables us to chain together multiple operations to perform complex tasks efficiently. Let's explore the possibilities:

a. INSERT INTO... SELECT:

This powerful construct allows you to combine the insertion and selection operations. You can insert data into a table directly from another table or a subquery. This technique facilitates data transformation and dynamic population during insertion.

b. UPDATE... FROM:

SQL enables you to leverage the data from one table to update records in another table. By combining the UPDATE statement with a subquery or another table, you can perform intricate updates based on specific conditions or join criteria.

c. DELETE... FROM:

The combination of the DELETE statement with a subquery or another table empowers you to perform targeted deletions based on complex filtering conditions or join criteria.

By skillfully combining data manipulation operations, you unlock a new level of efficiency and complexity, allowing you to manipulate your data with surgical precision.

5. Transaction Management: Ensuring Integrity

In the world of databases, data integrity is paramount. SQL provides transaction management mechanisms to ensure that modifications to your data occur in a controlled and consistent manner. Here are the key concepts of transaction management:

a. ACID Properties:
Transactions adhere to the ACID principles - Atomicity, Consistency, Isolation, and Durability. These principles ensure that each transaction is treated as a single, indivisible unit of work, guaranteeing data integrity and reliability.

b. COMMIT:
The COMMIT statement marks the successful completion of a transaction, persisting the changes made within the transaction to the database. It signifies

that the modifications are permanent and can be safely shared with other users.

c. ROLLBACK:

In case of errors or undesired outcomes, the ROLLBACK statement allows you to revert the changes made within a transaction. It returns the data to its state before the transaction began, ensuring that no unintended consequences persist.

d. SAVEPOINT:

SAVEPOINTs enable you to create intermediate checkpoints within a transaction. They provide a mechanism for partial rollback, allowing you to undo specific parts of a transaction without discarding the entire operation.

By mastering the art of transaction management, you safeguard the integrity of your data, ensuring that modifications occur in a controlled and consistent manner.

As we conclude this chapter on manipulating data with SQL, you now possess a formidable toolkit to shape and mold your data to your will. Whether you are inserting new records, updating existing information, deleting obsolete data, or combining operations to perform intricate tasks, SQL empowers you to wield the power of data manipulation with finesse and precision.

Remember, the true artistry lies not only in the technical execution of these operations but also in the thoughtful consideration of data integrity, efficiency, and organization. Embrace the power of data manipulation, and let your SQL skills shine as you unlock the full potential of your databases.

Chapter 5:

Best Practices and Beyond

Congratulations on reaching the advanced level of SQL mastery! In this chapter, we will explore the best practices, tips, and tricks that will elevate your SQL skills to new heights. Whether you are a beginner looking to expand your knowledge or an experienced professional seeking to optimize your queries, this chapter will provide you with the necessary tools to become an SQL guru.

Section 1: Writing Efficient Queries for Improved Performance

Writing efficient queries is crucial for optimizing the performance of your SQL applications. In this section, we will delve into various techniques to enhance query speed and reduce resource consumption. We will cover:

a. Choosing the Right Indexes:

Understand the importance of indexes and learn how to select the appropriate ones for your queries. We will discuss primary keys, unique keys, clustered and non-clustered indexes, and their impact on performance.

b. Query Tuning:
Dive into the world of query optimization by analyzing execution plans, identifying bottlenecks, and utilizing query hints and optimizer tricks to enhance query performance.

c. Join Optimization:
Master the art of joining tables efficiently by selecting the appropriate join types, utilizing join hints, and optimizing join conditions. We will explore inner joins, outer joins, cross joins, and self-joins.

Section 2: Understanding Query Optimization Techniques

To take your SQL skills to the next level, it's essential to have a deep understanding of query optimization techniques. In this section, we will explore advanced strategies to fine-tune your queries and improve overall performance. We will cover:

a. Subquery Optimization:
Discover the power of subqueries and learn how to optimize them using techniques such as rewriting subqueries as joins, using EXISTS and NOT EXISTS operators, and applying appropriate filtering conditions.

b. Query Rewriting:
Explore the art of query rewriting to simplify complex queries, eliminate redundant calculations, and improve query performance. We will discuss common rewriting techniques such as using derived tables, CTEs (Common Table Expressions), and inline views.

c. Query Caching:
Learn about query caching mechanisms offered by database management systems and leverage them to reduce query execution time and improve scalability.

Section 3: Working with Views and Stored Procedures

Views and stored procedures are powerful constructs in SQL that can enhance productivity and code reusability. In this section, we will explore best practices for working with views and stored procedures. We will cover:

a. Creating and Managing Views: Understand the benefits of using views and learn how to create and manage them effectively. We will discuss materialized views, indexed views, and view maintenance.

b. Designing and Optimizing Stored Procedures: Master the art of designing efficient and maintainable stored procedures. We will cover parameterization, transaction management, error handling, and optimizing stored procedure execution.

Section 4: Handling Errors and Troubleshooting Common Issues

In the world of SQL, errors and issues are bound to occur. The key is knowing how to handle them effectively. In this section, we will explore strategies for error handling and troubleshooting common SQL issues. We will cover:

a. Error Handling Techniques:
Learn how to gracefully handle errors in your SQL code, including using TRY...CATCH blocks, raising custom errors, and logging error information for debugging purposes.

b. Query Performance Analysis:
Discover tools and techniques for analyzing query performance, including interpreting execution plans, using SQL Profiler, and leveraging database monitoring and tuning utilities.

c. Common Performance Issues and Solutions:
Explore common performance bottlenecks in SQL applications and learn practical solutions to address them. We will cover issues such as inefficient queries,

locking and blocking, and excessive resource consumption.

Section 5: Resources for Further Learning and Exploration

To continue your SQL journey and stay updated with the latest advancements, it's essential to have access to valuable resources. In this section, we will provide a curated list of books, online courses, websites, and communities that can help you expand your SQL knowledge and connect with fellow enthusiasts.

By following the best practices, tips, and tricks outlined in this chapter, you will be well-equipped to optimize your SQL skills and tackle complex SQL challenges with confidence. Remember, SQL is a continuously evolving field, so never stop exploring and expanding your knowledge. With dedication and practice, you will become a true master of SQL, unlocking the full potential of data manipulation and analysis.

Happy querying!

Chapter 6:

Crafting and Sculpting the Database Structure

Welcome to the final chapter of our book, where we embark on a journey to master the art of creating and modifying the structure of a database. In this chapter, we will explore the intricacies of SQL statements, guiding you through the process of creating tables, defining key relationships, modifying existing tables, optimizing performance with indexes, and ensuring data integrity through constraints. Prepare yourself to become a maestro in shaping and refining the heart of any database.

Section 1: Laying the Foundation with Tables

Creating tables is like laying the foundation of a grand architectural marvel. We will begin by understanding the importance of choosing appropriate data types for our columns and the impact they have on performance and storage efficiency. Dive into the realm of data types, from the basic integers and strings to the more advanced types like dates and timestamps. We will discuss the nuances of each type and the considerations to keep in mind while selecting them.

Section 2: Forging Relationships with Keys

Relationships are the pillars that connect tables and establish coherence within the database. We will delve into the concepts of primary and foreign keys, understanding their significance and how they enforce relationships between tables. Learn the art of creating primary keys to ensure uniqueness and integrity, as well as foreign keys to establish referential integrity across tables. Explore various scenarios where different types of key relationships are appropriate, such as one-to-one, one-to-many, and many-to-many.

Section 3: Reshaping the Structure with ALTER TABLE

Databases, like living organisms, evolve over time. To adapt to changing requirements, we must become adept at modifying the structure of existing tables. Enter the ALTER TABLE statement—the chisel in the hands of the database sculptor. We will learn how to add and drop columns, modify data types, and even rename tables. Discover advanced techniques to manipulate table structure without losing valuable data. Master the art of table alteration, and let your database adapt to the ever-changing needs of your applications.

Section 4: Fine-tuning Performance with Indexes

Efficiency is the key to any successful database. Indexes play a crucial role in optimizing performance by providing quick access to data. We will uncover the intricacies of creating indexes and explore different types such as clustered, non-clustered, and full-text indexes. Learn how to analyze query execution plans and identify opportunities for index creation. Discover advanced techniques like covering indexes and index partitioning, and witness the dramatic impact they have on query speed.

Section 5: Enforcing Integrity with Constraints

Data integrity is the foundation of any reliable database system. Constraints act as guardians, preventing data from falling into the abyss of inconsistency and corruption. We will explore the world of constraints, from the common ones like NOT NULL and UNIQUE to more complex ones like CHECK and FOREIGN KEY constraints. Understand their role in maintaining data quality and learn how to create, modify, and drop constraints. Dive into the world of cascading actions and witness the power of constraints in preserving data integrity.

Congratulations! You have now mastered the art of creating and modifying the structure of a database using SQL statements. With your newfound skills, you have become a true virtuoso in the world of database management. Remember, the key to creating a masterpiece lies not only in technical expertise but also in the ability to envision the end result. As you sculpt your databases, keep in mind the importance of designing efficient structures, establishing meaningful relationships, and ensuring data integrity.

Covering these six comprehensive chapters, "SQL Beginners Guide" I believe the book has provide you with a solid foundation in SQL and equip you with the necessary knowledge and skills to embark on your journey to becoming an SQL expert.

We hope you have enjoyed this journey, filled with valuable insights and practical knowledge. It's time to take what you have learned and apply it to your own database projects, creating works of art that will inspire and empower. Please share your experience and recommend this book to your family, friends, and colleagues. Your feedback and support will be valuable, so please consider rating the book if you found it valuable.